The Brooklyn Bridge

MIKAYA PRESS

NEW YORK

For the kids of P.S. 321 in Brooklyn
who inspired this book

OTHER BOOKS BY ELIZABETH MANN

The Great Pyramid
The Great Wall
Hoover Dam
The Panama Canal
The Roman Colosseum
Machu Picchu
Tikal
Empire State Building

Editor: Stuart Waldman
Design: Lesley Ehlers Design

Library of Congress Cataloging-in-Publication Data
Mann, Elizabeth, 1948-
The Brooklyn Bridge: a wonders of the world book/ by Elizabeth Mann: with illustrations by
Alan Witschonke.
p.   cm.
Summary: Describes the construction of the Brooklyn Bridge, from its conception by John
Roebling in 1852 through, after many setbacks, its final
completion under the direction of his son, Washington, in 1883.
ISBN 1-931414-16-5
1. Bridges, Suspension–New York (State)–New York–Design and
construction–Juvenile literature. 2. Brooklyn Bridge (New York,N.Y.)–History–Juvenile litera-
ture. 3. Roebling family–Juvenile literature. 4. Roebling, John Augustus, 1806-1869–Juvenile literature. 5. Roebling, Washington Augustus, 1837-1926–Juvenile literature. [1. Brooklyn
Bridge (New York, N.Y.)–History. 2. Bridges–Design and construction. 3. Roebling, John
Augustus, 1806-1869. 4. Roebling, Washington Augustus. 1837-1926. 5. Engineers.] 1.
Witschonke, Alan, 1953- ill. 11. Title.
TG25.N53M36 1996
624 .5097471–dc20   96-14752
                                                                      AC

First paperback edition, 2006

Printed in China

The Brooklyn Bridge

A WONDERS OF THE WORLD BOOK

BY ELIZABETH MANN

WITH ILLUSTRATIONS BY ALAN WITSCHONKE

MIKAYA PRESS

NEW YORK

In the winter of 1852, John Roebling and his 15-year-old son, Washington, were riding a Fulton Ferry boat across the East River from New York to Brooklyn. The day was bitterly cold. The ferry inched along, bumping against huge chunks of ice. The trip seemed to take forever. John paced up and down the deck.

"This ferry just isn't good enough, Washington!" he exclaimed. "There should be a bridge here."

John Roebling was an engineer. His specialty was building bridges. As he looked across the East River, he could picture the bridge that he wanted there. He knew that it would be the most important one he would ever build.

For years after that, John tried to convince people that his plan for a bridge across the East River was a good one. Many liked the idea, especially those who lived in Brooklyn. They knew that as long as they had to depend on ferry boats to reach New York, Brooklyn would never become an important city. But most people thought it was impossible to bridge the wide and powerful river.

FULTON FERRY PIER

NEW YORK

EAST RIVER

BROOKLYN

At that time, New York and Brooklyn were two different cities, separated by the East River. Today New York and Brooklyn are part of one city called New York.

7

John A. Roebling was born in 1806 in a small village in Germany. His father wanted him to work in his tobacco shop, but his mother encouraged him to study engineering. He became fascinated with bridges but was frustrated by the lack of opportunities to build them in Germany. He moved to America in 1831, where he became known as a brilliant engineer.
He built bridges and canals all over the country.
He also established a farming community and a successful cable making company. Although he did many things in his life, John Roebling will always be remembered as the designer of the Brooklyn Bridge.

John knew it would be difficult. There were many problems to solve. The bridge would have to be strong enough to withstand the swift currents and powerful winds of the East River. It could not get in the way of the hundreds of boats that traveled on the river every day. It had to be so high that the masts of tall sailing ships could easily pass under it. And it had to be long. The East River was nearly half a mile wide at that point. But John also knew about a type of bridge that could solve all these problems. It was called a *suspension bridge*.

In many bridges, like this one in London, the roadway rested on a series of solid supports. The supports had to be close together. A bridge like this across the East River would have needed many supports because the river is so wide. There wouldn't have been enough room for boats.

5. The suspender cables hold up the roadway.

6. The roadway.

Every suspension bridge is different, but they all work in basically the same way. The roadway doesn't rest on supports. Instead it hangs in the air, suspended from thick cables. Only two towers are needed to hold up the cables, and they can be placed far apart to keep the river open for boat traffic.

2. The towers hold up the main cables.

4. The main cables hold up the suspender cables.

1. The foundations support the towers.

3. The anchorages hold the ends of the main cables.

John had already built three famous suspension bridges. This one across the East River would be the longest one he ever designed, but he was confident that it would work. Unfortunately, the people of New York and Brooklyn didn't agree with him. The idea was new to them, and they were afraid of it.

Then came the winter of 1867. It was so cold that the East River froze solid! Ferry boats were stuck in the thick ice. The only way to cross the river was on skates. People in Brooklyn couldn't get to their jobs in New York. They were desperate. At last they were willing to listen to John Roebling's plan.

Washington A. Roebling was born in Pennsylvania in 1837, the oldest of 7 children. Like his father, he studied engineering in college. He joined the Union Army during the Civil War and was promoted to Colonel. He fell in love with Emily, his commanding officer's sister. After the war, he married Emily and went to work as his father's assistant, building bridges.

In June of 1869, John Roebling finished the design for the bridge. He and Washington climbed out onto the end of the Fulton Ferry pier in Brooklyn to look over the place in the river where work would begin. He was so intent on what he was doing that he ignored the shrill whistle of an approaching ferry. Washington shouted a warning, but his father couldn't move fast enough. The boat slammed into the pier, crushing John's foot before he could jump out of the way. The injury became badly infected. He died a month later.

John's sudden death was a shock to everyone. Washington was especially sad. He was very close to his father and had shared his dream of a bridge across the East River. Now the dream was in danger, and he was the only one who could keep it alive. Although he was young and inexperienced, he decided he had to carry on the work his father had started. He accepted the job of Chief Engineer of the Brooklyn Bridge.

The caissons were built at a shipyard on the East River. Washington knew that boat builders would be able to seal the wood and make it waterproof. He didn't want any leaks while men were working under the river inside the caissons.

Washington began immediately. He had to build foundations under the water to support the bridge towers. If he built them on the muddy river bottom, they could slip, and the bridge would not be safe. He had to build them on a solid surface. He had to dig down through the mud to reach bedrock. To do this, he used enormous wooden boxes called caissons. The caissons sat on the river bottom and protected the workers inside them as they dug.

Washington had seen caissons used for small bridges in Europe, but the ones for the Brooklyn Bridge had to be much bigger. Imagine a building three stories tall and big enough to cover much of a city block. Imagine that the top two stories were made of solid wood, and that the building had no floor. That's what Washington's caissons looked like.

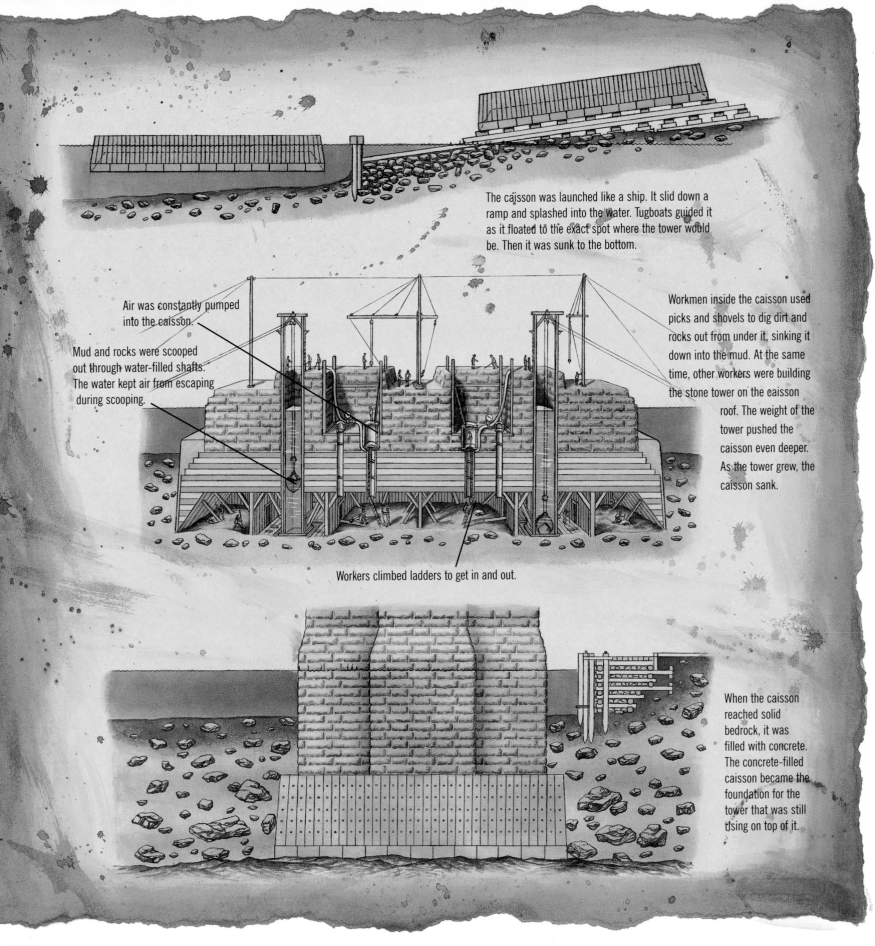

The caisson was launched like a ship. It slid down a ramp and splashed into the water. Tugboats guided it as it floated to the exact spot where the tower would be. Then it was sunk to the bottom.

Air was constantly pumped into the caisson.

Mud and rocks were scooped out through water-filled shafts. The water kept air from escaping during scooping.

Workmen inside the caisson used picks and shovels to dig dirt and rocks out from under it, sinking it down into the mud. At the same time, other workers were building the stone tower on the caisson roof. The weight of the tower pushed the caisson even deeper. As the tower grew, the caisson sank.

Workers climbed ladders to get in and out.

When the caisson reached solid bedrock, it was filled with concrete. The concrete-filled caisson became the foundation for the tower that was still rising on top of it.

The Brooklyn caisson was built first, and the digging inside it went on for months. One evening a messenger raced to Washington's house. He pounded on the door with an urgent message: a fire had started deep inside the thick wooden roof of the caisson. If it continued to burn, the roof would weaken and the tower would crash through it. Washington hurried back to the bridge and stayed all night helping to put the fire out. No matter what they did, the high pressure air in the caisson just made the fire burn hotter. In desperation, Washington opened the doors in the top of the caisson and pumped it full of river water. Finally the fire was extinguished, but Washington collapsed and was carried to his home. He had suffered a severe attack of caisson disease.

Caisson disease was a constant danger for Washington and his workers. The weight of the river water on a caisson was tremendous, and the air inside was under great pressure. Every day when their work was done, the men climbed from the high pressure beneath the river to the normal air pressure outside. They didn't know that their bodies needed time to adjust to the pressure change, and some became ill. Going to work was scary for the men because they didn't know why or when the mysterious pains and paralysis would strike. Many quit because of it. Nowadays we call it the bends – deep sea divers sometimes get it when they swim to the surface too quickly–and we know how to prevent it and cure it.

In 1871, the Brooklyn caisson reached solid bedrock at 44 1/2 feet below the river. The workmen climbed out for the last time, and the caisson was filled with concrete. The first foundation was finished.

On the New York side of the river, they were not so lucky. The caisson sank deeper and deeper below the river without reaching solid rock. Fifty feet. Many men were suffering from caisson disease. Sixty feet. Still no bedrock. Hundreds of workers quit. One man died of the disease, and then another. Washington was horrified. If the digging continued, more men would die. If he stopped the digging before the caisson rested on a solid surface, the tower might tip. He didn't want to risk workers' lives *or* the safety of the bridge. He had to make the most difficult decision of his life.

Washington worked day and night doing tests on the soil beneath the caisson. He discovered that it was hard-packed sand and gravel, a very solid surface. He concluded that it could support the bridge tower. The caisson was at 78 $\frac{1}{2}$ feet below the river when he gave the command,

"Stop digging!"

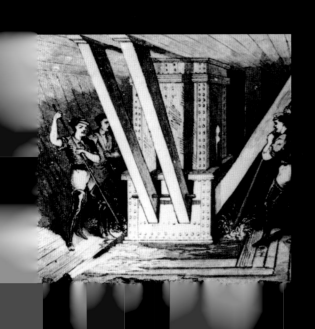

One hundred men at a time worked in the hot, humid caissons. The pressurized air was difficult to breathe and candles gave only dim light. It was exhausting, dirty work. The pay was $2 a day.

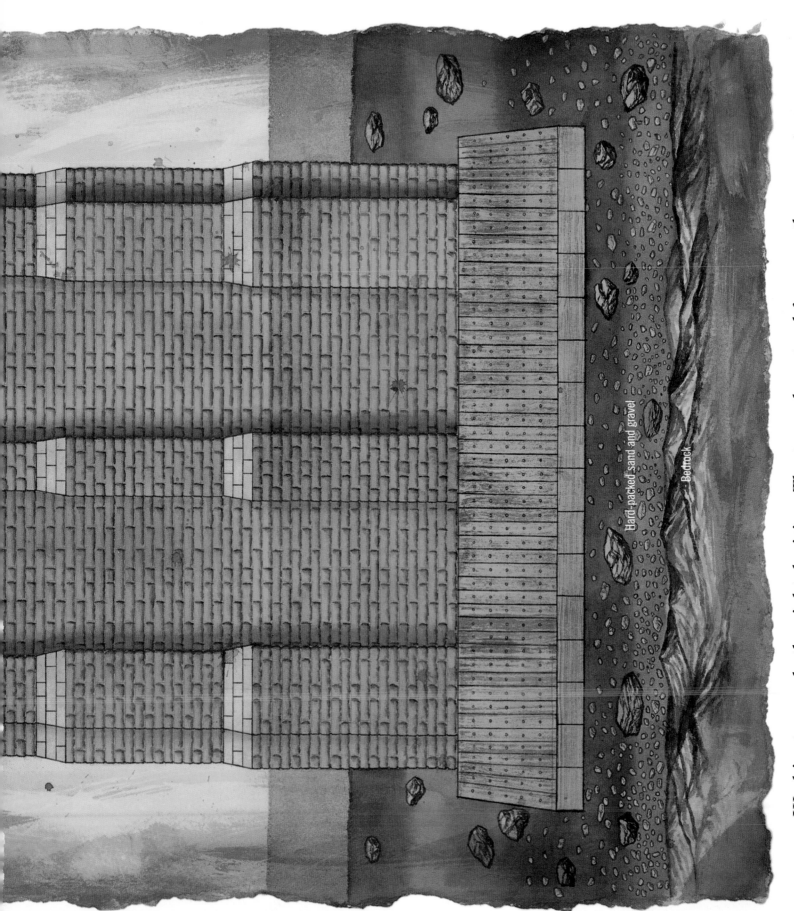

Hard-packed sand and gravel

Bedrock

Washington made the right decision. The tower has stood for more than a century.

The foundation has not slipped.

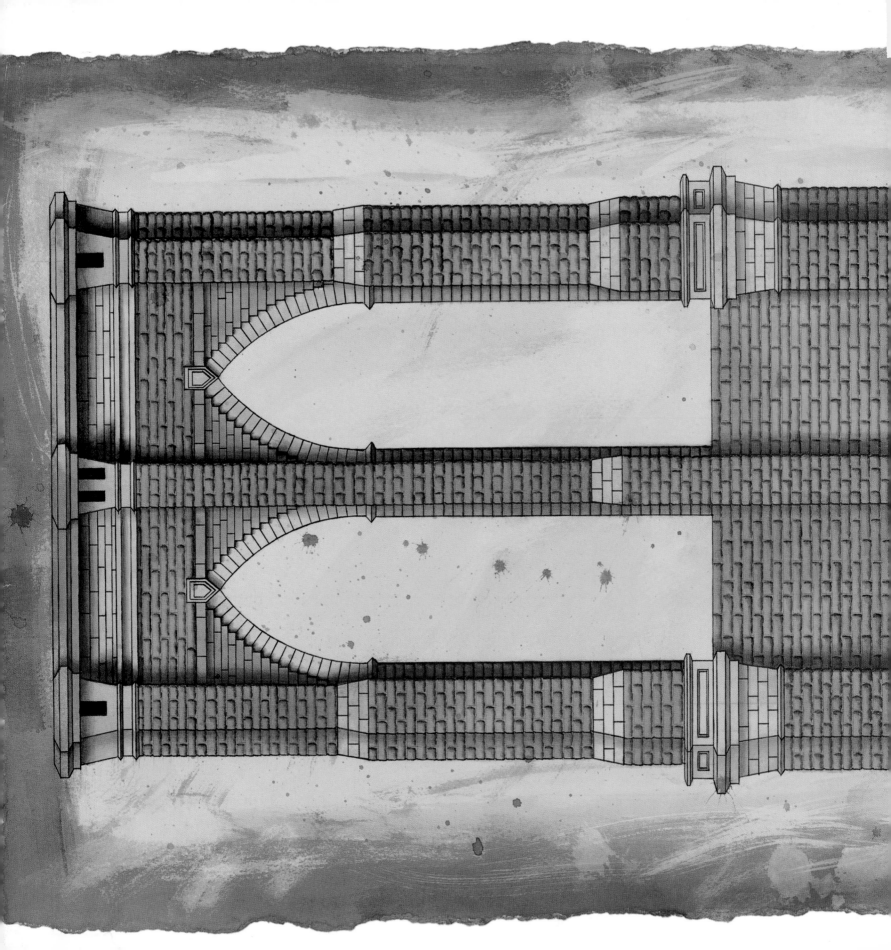

Washington's house was in Brooklyn Heights, not far from the East River. His bedroom faced the bridge.

Washington spent many hours in the caisson during this difficult time, and it made his disease even worse. Again he was rushed to his home, doubled over in terrible pain. This time the attack was so bad that he couldn't recover. He never returned to the bridge. From then on his only view of the construction was through binoculars from his bedroom window.

Emily Warren was born in 1843 in Cold Springs, New York. She was known for her quick wit and common sense. After her marriage, she and Washington traveled through Europe to study new ways of building bridges. On that trip she gave birth to her only child, John Roebling II. He was born in Germany, right across the street from the house where his grandfather, John Roebling, had grown up.

Work continued, thanks to Washington's wife Emily Roebling. She was his only contact with the world outside his sickroom. She carried his instructions to the men on the bridge and brought him progress reports. She talked with him about the work and became involved in making important decisions. In many ways, she took over for him. It would have been a challenge for anyone, but it was especially hard for Emily. At that time, women never worked on construction projects.

Emily was not an engineer, but she had learned a lot about suspension bridges from Washington and John. That knowledge, as well as her intelligence and calm manner, helped her to overcome the prejudice against her. She won the respect of all the workers. They realized how important she was to the building of the bridge.

This old photograph shows the Brooklyn tower under construction in 1872. It's less than half finished, but already it makes everything around it seem tiny.

The digging in the caissons had been carried out almost in secret. Only the workers really knew of the difficult and remarkable work that was done in those underwater rooms and of the terrible hardships they endured.

The construction of the towers was very different. Every day thousands of people watched in amazement from ferries and docks as three tall cranes, powered by noisy steam engines, hoisted each huge stone block high into the air and swung it into position.

Excitement mounted as the towers grew taller. Since most buildings then were less than 5 stories high, the 25-story towers must have seemed stupendous.

The completed tower was the tallest thing around. The view of New York Harbor from the top had never been seen before.

Once the towers were finished, the two anchorages were built. A giant tug of war is constantly happening in a suspension bridge. The heavy roadway pulls down on the main cables, but the anchorages hold them firmly and keep them from sagging. Each anchorage weighed 120,000,000 pounds. That's like having 12,000 large elephants hanging on to the main cables.

The wide, thin scaffoldings were called cradles. Workers stood on them during cable spinning to make sure each wire curved exactly the same.

Next, thousands of thin steel wires were strung from Brooklyn to New York. It was called spinning cable. Bundles of wires were wrapped together to make four main cables. Each cable contained over 3,500 miles of steel wire, enough to stretch from Brooklyn to Los Angeles.

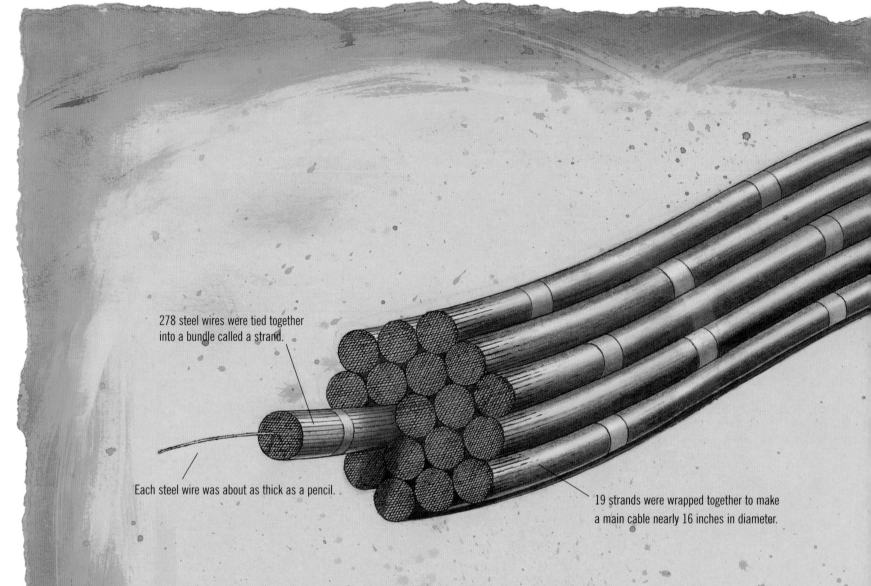

278 steel wires were tied together into a bundle called a strand.

Each steel wire was about as thick as a pencil.

19 strands were wrapped together to make a main cable nearly 16 inches in diameter.

This was the first time that a bridge had been built with steel cables. Before that, iron cables, chains, or even rope had been used, and there had been disastrous results. Bridges had collapsed because of weak cables. Washington wanted to make sure that his bridge was not a disaster. He chose to use steel because it is stronger than iron. It was another wise decision. Since then, only steel has been used in bridge construction.

ROEBLING'S
Steel and Iron

WIRE ROPE

Of Every Kind and for Every Purpose. Suspension Bridge
Cables a Specialty.

Covington and Cincinnati Suspension Bridge, built by John A. Roebling. Main Span 1,057 feet.

John Roebling started his wire rope
company in a farm shed in 1841.
By 1871, it was the largest one in the
country. Most of the steel wire used in
the Brooklyn Bridge came from the
Roebling factories.

In August, 1876 hundreds of boats and thousands of people gathered to watch as Master Mechanic Frank Farrington glided from Brooklyn to Manhattan on a tiny swing attached to the first wire. He waved from his shaky seat and the crowd below cheered wildly. It was the first trip across the Brooklyn Bridge!

The elaborate construction project in the East River attracted even more attention while the cables were being spun. Even the most doubtful critics had to believe that the bridge would really be built. Newspapers and magazines in America and Europe wrote many articles about it. Politicians made speeches about it. The Brooklyn Bridge was the biggest show in town!

A wooden footbridge was built for the workers to use. Word of the fantastic views from it spread quickly, and tourists came from all over to walk out on it. Standing hundreds of feet above a deep, fast moving river on a swaying, narrow footbridge was a thrilling adventure for some. For others it was a little too exciting. People panicked, fainted, and had to be carried back down. The footbridge had to be closed to the public.

Cable work was done from small wooden perches that hung high above the East River. Sailors were often hired because they were used to working on the masts of tall sailing ships. They were able to hang on tight when the wind blew, and they weren't frightened when they looked down at the water far below. Not too frightened, anyway.

Although the men were skillful and very careful, accidents still happened. One of the most serious occurred when a strand broke loose. It whipped through the air, killing two men, injuring others, and narrowly missing a crowded ferry boat. Altogether, including John Roebling, 21 men died working on the Brooklyn Bridge.

The steel floor beams were attached to the ends of the suspender cables. The beams were bolted together and reinforced to stiffen the roadway so that it wouldn't move in the wind. The footbridge, where the two men are standing, was taken down when the bridge was finished.

The towers and anchorages were finished. The four main cables were in place. All that remained to be done was to hang the roadway from the main cables. Steel suspender cables were used for this. The suspenders were attached at the top to the main cables, and at the bottom to steel floor beams. Then the beams were bolted to each other to make a strong, stiff roadway floor. The roads, train tracks, and pedestrian walkway would all be built on this floor.

Washington strengthened the bridge even more by adding extra cables called diagonal stays. Diagonal stays had not been in his father's original plan, but Washington wanted to make sure that even heavy railroad trains could cross the Brooklyn Bridge safely. When it was finished, the bridge was six times stronger than it needed to be.

Safety and strength were not the only things that John Roebling thought about when he designed the Brooklyn Bridge. He believed the people of New York and Brooklyn deserved a bridge that was as beautiful as he could make it. The elegant high arches of the stone towers, the graceful swoop of the main cables, and the pattern created by the suspender cables and the diagonal stays made the bridge very lovely indeed. John even raised the walkway above the level of the road so pedestrians had a view of New York Harbor that was as breathtaking as the bridge itself.

Electric lamps, like the one at the left of the picture, lined the bridge. Electricity had never been used to light a bridge before. At night it looked quite magical.

On May 24, 1883, the Brooklyn Bridge was opened. Stores, businesses, and even the Brooklyn schools were closed for the day. People came from all over the country to be part of the opening ceremony. Washington Roebling peered through his binoculars as Chester A. Arthur, president of the United States, walked across the bridge from New York to meet Emily on the Brooklyn side.

That night, there was a great party in honor of the Roeblings' beautiful bridge. Hundreds of thousands of people cheered for over an hour as fireworks exploded from the towers. New York had never before had such a grand celebration!

Washington and Emily watched the fireworks from their bedroom window. After 14 years the long struggle was over. Their bridge was done.

Emily returned happily to a busy life away from the bridge. She gave large parties and traveled all around the United States and Europe. She went back to school and earned her law degree when she was 55 years old. For a woman living at that time it was a remarkable accomplishment.

For Emily Roebling it was not at all surprising.

Washington slowly recovered from his long illness. He worked in the family business, making steel wire for bridges all over the country. He lived quietly at home, playing music, collecting rocks and minerals, and writing long letters to his beloved son John. When he spoke of the Brooklyn Bridge, he said that it had been a time of great suffering for him. He died in 1926 at the age of 89.

THE BROOKLYN BRIDGE

Total length of roadway	5,989 feet
Length of river span between towers	1,595 $1/2$ feet
Height of roadway above water in center of river span	135 feet
Depth of Brooklyn caisson below water	44 $1/2$ feet
Depth of New York caisson below water	78 $1/2$ feet
Height of towers above water	276 $1/2$ feet
Diameter of each main cable	15 $3/4$ inches
Number of wires in each main cable	5,434

INDEX

CREDITS

Author's Collection: pp. 6-7, 9, 12-13, 28-29, 37

Corbis: pp. 20-21

Library of Congress: pp. 44-45

Museum of the City of New York: pp. 28 (top), 31, 33 (top), 35 (top), 40–41

Rensselaer Polytechnic Institute, Archives and Special Collections: pp. 8, 14, 16, 30, 34, 35 (bottom), 42

Rutgers University: p. 26

Alan Witschonke: pp. 4, 10-11, 15, 17, 19, 22-23, 24, 27, 32-33, 38-39, 43